HOW TO TELL IF YOUR MAN IS

Gay

A WOMAN'S GUIDE

BY DE'MEK LEVON

How To Tell If Your Man Is Gay: *A Woman's Guide*
Copyright © 2018 Demetrice Ross. All rights reserved.

Unless otherwise indicated, all scripture quotations are taken from the King James Version of the Bible.

Author: De'Mek Levon | Demek__levon@yahoo.com

ISBN: 978-0-692-15732-9

Category: Marriage / Dating / Relationships / Divorce

Library of Congress Cataloging-in-Publication Data

Publishing Consultant: Leandrea Rivers Owens (laowens.com)

Editor: Barbara Joe (Amanipublishing@gmail.com)

Cover Design: Barbara Upshaw-Mayers | Aura Graphics & Design

Formatting Designer: Eli Blyden | Eli-The Book Guy

Printed in the United States of America

This book is dedicated to my beautiful Mother

JENNIFER D. ROSS

3-9-60 – 12-25-14

May you **Rest in Peace**

Table of Contents

LETTER TO THE READER

I chose to write this particular type of book to enlighten the female population, who's been indirectly or directly, affected by an undercover or down low man.

At the age of seven, I discovered I was same-sex oriented. By the age of twelve, I'd become sexually active with other boys. Since then, I've engaged in numerous tryst (discreet get-togethers and encounters with "out" gay men like myself to the so-called heterosexual straight man).

Through my experiences with other men, I've learned that many women are affected and blindsided by the secret lives their significant others, spouses, and companions are living. I feel that it is important to inform as many women as I can through my book to spare them from the inevitable heartbreak and disappointment they'll experience upon discovering the homosexual infidelity of the men they love.

After twenty years of living this lifestyle, I felt it was time to educate all women and expose the executive businessmen, professional athletes, construction workers, drug dealers, alpha males, husbands, boyfriends, and baby daddies of their deceitful intentions.

I hope that, as a reader, you will gain enough knowledge through the information contained in this book to be able to distinguish a true heterosexual straight man from the so-called straight man.

I did not gain my knowledge from any Ivy League school or major institutional research or study. All the information contained within this book is based on real-life experiences. This book is not intended for a certain type of woman based on race, religion, status, or caliber. This is for all women. Ladies, this is your guide. Use it and refer to it as needed.

Enjoy,

De'Mek Lavon

HOW TO TELL IF YOUR MAN IS

Gay

A WOMAN'S GUIDE

INTRODUCTION

There are as many different sexual preferences as there are races and religions. Of course, the most common preference in today's society is man and woman. People tend to think this is the way we were created, so a heterosexual relationship is the way we all shall live. What about those who live and prefer a different lifestyle? Is their preference or way of life an incorrect way to live?

Although a heterosexual relationship may be the most common union between two people, there are other unions and relationships that are just as relevant in society. Homosexuality is one of the larger preferred sexual preferences in today's society. It is also the most hated and ridiculed preference. The constant discrimination is due largely to others not fully understanding the life of a homosexual or the lifestyle of the Lesbian Gay Bisexual Transgender and Queen (LGBTQ) community.

Due to the rapid growth in homosexual relationships, the ability for a woman to find a straight man has become more complicated than ever. I'm constantly hearing the opinion of many women that, "There's a shortage of good men," or "There are not enough good men to go around." These opinions couldn't be any further from the truth. There's no such thing as a shortage of good men.

There are plenty of decent men to accommodate good women. You have to know who to choose and how to choose, and how to distinguish a straight man from a gay one!

During the course of this book, I will do my best to educate you on the characteristics and behavior of a straight man who may be indulging in homosexuality or living an undercover lifestyle. Remember, indulging in homosexuality doesn't prevent him from being a man, it only alters his sexuality. His appearance, masculine swagger, and arrogant demeanor will remain intact.

Unfortunately, men are no longer taken by the physical beauty of a woman. Sorry, ladies, but physical beauty and a big booty can no longer contain a man's interest in you. Technique is what he's needing, and that technique is from a man. It's been said that, "One's very own sex is better at pleasing than the opposite gender."

Gay relationships, whether open or undercover, are in full effect and growing fast. It's kind of like this: you know you're on a strict no carb diet but decide that one small piece of chocolate cake couldn't possibly hurt or disrupt your diet. If you indulge in the eating of that one piece of cake, then you'll continue to have another and another. Before you know it, your diet is over, and you're full fledge indulging.

Meaning, if a man so much as consider having an affair with another man, then the percentage in straight men will continue to slowly diminish. This book will not only make it easier for you to distinguish the real from the fake but also make it easier to find a good straight man. If you're sure you have a good man, then keep him; but for those women who are not so sure if they're sleeping with a man who's wearing a mask, it's about time we unmask him.

"How to tell if your man is gay" is a woman's guide.

"What's done in the dark will always come to the light."

F. O. G.
FACES OF GAY

I t's imperative that you are aware of all the different types of men associated with the LGBTQ lifestyle. How would you know if your man is gay if you didn't know what type of face he's displaying? Normally, people would look at being gay as happy, lively, and flamboyant. Those days are long gone. Gay has taken on a new face. An undetachable face! Gay is now masculine, egotistic, cocky, and downright arrogant.

The days of being able to spot a gay man, or one you may assume is gay, are over. Every day, whether by blogs, social media, or the news, men are coming out of the closet and revealing their true sexualities.

We always seem to act surprised when the reality is he'd been wearing his face the entire time. Ladies, you're the ones who are missing the signs and not recognizing these faces. Take a long look at your male construction workers, drug dealers, professional athletes, and jocks. Now ask yourself, is there a possibility that your man could be gay?

The days of suspecting your man is secretly having an affair with another woman are over. Not only do you have to worry about him sleeping with other women, you now have to worry about him sleeping with other men. If a man desires other men, then he should be with a man. Straddling the fence is cowardly and manipulative. Having a wife and children, but secretly indulging in homosexuality, is unfair to those women who love them and share a bed with them.

You may be under the impression that you have a decent man only to discover he's another man's lover. Don't be clueless or fooled by the face, masculine demeanor, or super sexy swagger anymore. Knowledge is power and knowing who and what you're dealing with is critical when dating, being intimate, or in a committed relationship with a man. If he's indulging in homosexual activity, he's most likely adept at keeping his exploits concealed. The heartbreak you'll experience will be extremely painful, so I'm going to try my best to prevent him from hurting you. Let's take a look at the different faces, positions, and roles men have in the LGBTQ lifestyle.

STRAIGHT MAN/DOWN LOW MAN

One who prefers to be in a relationship with a woman but secretly indulges in homosexuality. This particular type of man is masculine, arrogant, and smooth. He tends to feel he's not gay because of his preferred position as the giver in the bedroom rather than the receiver. Reality is that no matter what role or position he may be playing, if he's indulging, then he's gay. This classifies him as being on the down low and also known as a **trade**, which makes him the hardest to distinguish or detect.

TOP

This type of man is similar to the average straight man with masculine characteristics but has an open sexual preference. A **top** doesn't hide his attraction toward men, and he's strictly the man/giver in the relationship. He'll engage in sexual intercourse with a woman but prefers a bottom.

BOTTOMS

There are two types of **bottoms** in this category: a masculine and a feminine bottom. The masculine bottom is a guy who openly dates and prefers females, but he is the receiver and prefers other masculine men in homosexual relationships.

PUNKS, FAGS, QUEERS

These categories are all pretty much the same with different labels. These specific groups of guys are extremely lively and display flamboyant and feminine characteristics. Their sexual preferences are versatile, also referenced as **flip-floppers** (meaning they engage in either role).

VERSATILE BOTTOM

A versatile bottom is normally the one receiving. But on occasion, he can become a top, depending on the situation. Verse bottoms are not known to date females and prefer regular tops, straight men, or verse tops.

VERSATILE MAN

A fully versatile man displays masculine characteristics and has no preference. He's all around top to bottom, can be either or, and date men and women.

There are a few categories I didn't mention due to their obvious recognition. I'm sure you would know if your man were a drag queen or a transsexual. I'm hoping you could distinguish those characteristics. Now that you know and have a full understanding of what the many faces of gay consist of, you can decide which descriptive category your man may fit or belong to. If he's a so-called "straight man," then you can now decide what type of man he prefers.

The information provided in this chapter is substantial when trying to distinguish the straight man from the gay man. Just because you don't see the tendencies, it doesn't mean they don't exist. Don't be blinded or clueless. It's all in the know, so be knowledgeable because homosexuality can live in your home and your bed.

WHAT MAKES A MAN GAY

The most commonly asked question is how does someone become gay or what makes a person gay? There are many different reasons a person could become gay or just plain out be gay. The only difference between being gay and becoming gay is when and if that person decides to make it publicly known. In my opinion, a person is born gay. He can't go to bed a straight man at night and wake up a gay man the next morning. Trust me; it's more complicated than that.

Homosexuality is not an identity crisis. We, as people, don't get to decide if we're born with or without disabilities or disorders. We don't get to choose our sexual preference. The creator is solely responsible for our existence. What we can decide is how we choose to live our lives. We can accept the life we were given and be happy, or we can live in shame and hide our true identity from the world.

This is the only difference between men who are straight and the ones who are pretending. Although people find it hard to believe that someone can be born gay, it's the only theory that makes sense. Trust me, ladies, it's there from the beginning.

People tend to say or think that homosexuality is a demonic spirit. Those people are entitled to their opinions, and that's exactly why they're constantly making an ass out of themselves every fucking day. If homosexuality was, in fact, a demonic spirit—if that pathetic conclusion was the case, then why has this spirit never been heard to be removed from the body?

I'm sure it was attempted, but if one declares prayer or treatment changed their sexual preference, they're fucking lying! I've been openly gay my entire life. I've been through many different forms of counseling, prayed for countless times, and I'll be the first to truly tell you it does not work. I am who I am because this is who I was born to be. The men who are indulging in homosexuality, are only indulging in the lifestyle that was intended for them. They're afraid to fully be who they were born to be because they can't accept it and feel as though society won't accept it.

Some guys blame their homosexuality on something devastating that took place in their childhood like rape or molestation. This could likely be true but very unlikely. While this is a sad reason, it's also a sad excuse and a way for men to look for people to accept them for who they really are. They try to justify their homosexuality with pity stories. When the truth is, they were gay long before any tragic event took place. So the rape and molestation stories don't move me, and it's a bunch of bullshit.

If I were a man who had been a victim of rape or molestation as a child, there's absolutely no way I would embrace a lifestyle that tormented my childhood. That would be like revisiting that painful part of my life over and over again. A man uses this excuse often to get a woman to feel obligated to respect his decision to be gay. Don't rule out the possibility that he may have been molested, but I can assure you that's not what made him homosexual or turned him gay. If anything, he would dislike homosexuals not become another man's lover. Think about it, ladies, it doesn't make sense.

Another reason they give is hanging around females or being raised by women. This is one of the craziest excuses I've ever heard and one of the most ridiculous. How can being around the opposite sex change another's sexual preference? There's plenty of men who have all female siblings, and they're not gay! What about all the men who were raised by women? That's an insult to the women who raised men or to every woman raising a son single-handedly.

Again, this is a cowardly way for a man to justify his homosexuality. A man will never accept the fact that he was born gay and feels others will never accept the fact that he was born gay and feels others will never respect that as being true. You may ask yourself, "If a man is born gay, and meant to be that way, then why is he attracted to women?" From the heart of a gay man, being discriminated on is harder than actually being openly gay. Hated, disliked, and ridiculed for being who you were born to be is enough to make you want to commit suicide.

There was a time in my life when I was tired of the hate and seriously considered dating women to prevent the pain I experienced from living an alternate lifestyle. The constant stares and disgusted looks on people's faces when they realized my sexual preference was different from theirs was enough to push me into a dark place. It took courage and strength to come out and stand tall to reveal the real me.

It's so much hatred and negativity concerning homosexuality; it makes them want to keep it a secret forever. So instead of living for themselves, men attempt to live for society and what it views as correct. This forces them to keep their true sexual preference a secret, all the while dating women and ultimately destroying their lives. It's hard to imagine that these men would intentionally sacrifice the lives of women to protect their own. But, the truth is, they will. Their reputations are far more important than the women will ever be.

"A man who carries condoms is certainly guilty of infidelity. Heterosexual men, or so-called straight men, tend to think they're immune from contracting an incurable sexually transmitted disease from a woman, so they prefer unprotected sex with women. If your man is indulging in homosexuality, he'll be sure to try and protect himself by wearing protection;

thus, he's carrying condoms."

SEX

Sex is always a sure way to know when your man is being unfaithful. Either he's not as passionate and attentive as he once was, or he's just not putting out or showing any interest. Nevertheless, when your sex life goes down the drain, so does your relationship. When a man is dealing with a normal case of infidelity, his sexual desires will change.

When he's dealing with infidelity involving homosexuality not only will he experience changes in his sexual desires, but his sexual appetite and sexual performance will also undergo significant changes. Those changes will reflect that of an alternate lifestyle. Only you will be able to distinguish the difference between the two.

If your man is having an affair with another woman, you really won't notice the drastic change in his sexual performance, due largely to him still being physically and sexually attracted to women. Pleasing a woman would still be his desire. If you were to notice a change in his sexual performance, due to his infidelity, it would simply be because he's not sexually attracted to you anymore.

A woman is more sensual during sex than a man. She prefers to be touched, gently caressed, and stroked at a gentle but steady pace. However, men prefer more dominant sex. Their bodies are harder and can endure more of a sexual beating. If you're noticing your man is not as attentive and gentle to your body as he once was and now prefers rougher and more aggressive sex, there's a great possibility he's sleeping with another man.

If he is indeed engaging in sexual intercourse with another man, his appetite has definitely changed. When changes occur in a man's sexual appetite, you will notice the changes. If your man is doing things he wouldn't normally do or requesting you perform things he wouldn't normally require of you, then you should be concerned.

I'm going to be blunt pertaining to what I have to say because I need you to fully understand the information I'm relying to you. A lot of women enjoy anal sex, but there are those who don't. If anal sex is something that has never been incorporated into your sex life, but now out of the blue he's requesting it, then one of two things has happened: Either he's curious about what it would feel like to penetrate a guy but chooses to experiment with you before exploring his curiosity, or he's already been exposed to homosexuality.

If he's doing things like eating or licking your anus, then he's certainly been exposed to homosexuality. A man will indulge in the eating of your vagina because it's supposed to be eaten. But eating your asshole is a completely different ballgame. Some men enjoy performing this type of oral sex on their women, but that percentage is minute. In fact, the majority of men find it to be quiet disgusting. It takes one hell of an appetite to stomach the eating of one's anus. It takes the stomach of a gay man to find pleasure and enjoyment in this type of oral sex. If this is something he enjoys, then he's gay with no further investigation needed.

Another way to determine if your man is gay is through his sexual performance while giving him oral sex. If he's positioning himself during oral sex so that his anus is exposed, or in plain sight, then that's a clear indication that he prefers to have his asshole fingered while receiving oral sex. He won't just come out, and say, "Ahh, yeah, baby; finger fuck me." That would certainly kill the mood and raise immediate suspicion. So, the actual invitation can happen a few different ways. You won't even realize you have been invited. It'll be cunning, swift, and undetectable.

If he's lying on his back while you're performing oral sex, and he's lifting his legs to expose his third eye, or standing while receiving oral sex, and lifts one leg unto the bed, couch or chair to give you access, then that's an indication he enjoys ejaculation by a technique called "milking the prostate." This sexual technique is performed while masturbating or receiving oral sex.

A finger is inserted into the anus and then curled as if you were saying, "Come here." This applies pressure to his prostate gland, forcing him to cum harder and faster. Believe it or not, it's a man's G-spot and a lot of men prefer to ejaculate this way, especially gay men.

When a man attempts to explore his sexuality with you, it's his last attempt to see if you can fulfill his sexual needs at home before he leaves your ass for Tyrone. If you can't satisfy his desires and fulfill his fantasies, then you will lose his attention altogether. That doesn't necessarily mean he'll leave you for a man. It just means he'll be there physically, but mentally and sexually, he'll be elsewhere.

Then we have the tossing of your man's salad. For those of you who need me to elaborate, I'm talking about eating your man's ass. I know just the thought of it makes you come near vomiting. But believe it or not, some women indulge in ass eating. I know a few of them personally. The thought of having a man bent over grabbing his ankles while having his salad tossed is a disturbing image, and something you wouldn't see every day unless that man is gay. This sexual position would be extremely uncomfortable and inappropriate for a straight man.

The women, who are indulging in this type of sexual activity with their men, are obviously aware of his homosexuality but clearly don't mind. That's okay; it's their bedrooms and their sex lives. This book is not for those women who are okay with their men indulging in homosexuality. It's for those women who are not and lack the knowledge to distinguish real heterosexual men from fake heterosexual men. If you want to know, then pay close attention to his sexual performance. His body language during sex will speak for itself. If you miss the indication, you'll certainly miss the revelation. It's entirely up to you. It's your man and your sex life. The choice is yours.

"Wearing dark-colored shades or low fitted hats are ways for an undercover man to conceal his identity. Request that he remove his disguises and watch his insecurities flare up, displaying negative reactions."

FEAR

To be afraid of unpleasant emotions caused by expectation or awareness of danger is a major factor in the world of undercover men. The coming out factor for any undercover man is like carrying a huge secret around for years. If it's ever revealed, it could ultimately destroy or result in the loss of everything that means the most to you, including family, friends, relationships, and sometimes job.

That's a lot to lose for just one little secret. So, because everything a man holds dear to his heart is at stake, he's cautious when choosing his sexual dealings. If you're in a committed relationship with a man who's having an affair with another man, he's what we consider or refer to as a **trade**: A discreet down low man in a committed relationship with a woman but secretly sleeping with other men. Men who are a trade are particular in the way they move. Their whole objective is to be **unclockable**, hard to read or distinguish. They want to stay clear of the possibility of being **sprayed**, unmasked or made aware of.

In the opinion of an undercover man being involved with a punk/fag, one who display's feminine characteristics, could result in him being sprayed. The more flamboyant a man is, the more likely he is to do the things that females do, like gossip. So, it is almost forbidden for an undercover or down low man to be sexually involved with a flamboyant guy unless he's in jail or prison, then the rules slightly change.

These men are so fearful of being detected as gay that they usually date or sleep with men who are similar to themselves—one who has a girlfriend, wife, and children. This way, you nor anyone else will ever suspect their relationship to be anything more than normal between two guys. This friend is normally the one who's always around, attends all the family functions, and the one who's apart of his life just as much as you are. I know you're probably saying, "No fucking way," while thinking about this one guy who's always around. Trust me, ladies, these men are playing the game this way to save their images and reputations.

One day, my friend and I had our minds and pockets set on shopping. To my unfortunate surprise, she couldn't find her car keys. We searched the entire house but came up with nothing. She declined the offer to take my car, being that hers was recently purchased and updated with all the newest features. She's a high class, dependent female who has been given the best of everything at the expense of her hood rich, drug dealing boyfriend. She wasn't aware that everything came with a price, including love. I insisted again that we take my car, but she refused. She called her boyfriend a few times to no avail; it angered her that he wasn't answering his phone.

"Take me to the spot," she said. The spot, being the location where drugs were manufactured and sometimes sold. I almost refused; but seeing her frustration, I decided antagonizing her wouldn't help the situation. I didn't need directions because I'd been to the spot-on previous occasions when we were out and about. She'd stop by momentarily to pick up money or drop off food. On each visit, the atmosphere was dead, no cars, movement, or life.

Everything about the location was discreet. I assumed the lack of activity lowered the possibility of being arrested. When we arrived, nothing seemed unusual or out of place. I parked the car and hit the engine. I'd never stepped foot inside and intended to keep my ass planted just as I'd done on every other visit. She exited the car and approached the house. She knocked on the door, but no one answered. She peeped through the window, but the curtains obstructed her view.

She pulled her phone from her pocket to call him again when a luxury SUV pulled into the driveway. By this time, I was agitated because instead of shopping, I was parked in front of a drug hole awaiting indictment. When the guy exited the vehicle, everything about him screamed "drug dealer," from his arrogant demeanor to the sway of his iced-out chain. She obviously knew him because they exchanged words. He produced a key, and they went inside. A few moments later, she reappeared, running out of the house, and screaming to the heavens above.

My heart immediately sank to my stomach. *Oh, my God; he's dead!* I looked past her to the house, and there he stood in the doorway in nothing but his socks, yelling after her. She was still crying and mumbling something inaudible, when she arrived at the car. Seeing her storming from the house the way she had, I was sure she'd found him dead. But there he was naked in the doorway. Then it hit me, *Naked? Cheating bastard!*

At that moment, my regard for her pain turned into anger. I was disgusted that she sat weeping over this cheating bastard when this was exactly what she'd signed up for. She thought that nice cars, expensive clothing, and jewelry came without a price. Everything comes with a price and the tag on love is the healthiest of them all.

Although I was disgusted with her for crying over this man, I felt her pain; cheating is always a painful experience. "Listen, don't waste your time crying over something you should obviously expect," I said. "Dee, he's a drug dealer and constantly in the streets. I expect him to cheat."

"What I didn't expect was to walk in and see another man's dick in his ass."

I had known for a few years that her man was gay. I had never seen him indulge, but I'd heard through a reliable source that he was an active player in the league. I'd never taken the initiative to tell her because I felt she would never believe me, and our friendship would have probably suffered and come to an end from my accusations.

She was completely blinded by the things he had given her, obviously, for that purpose. I had to let her discover his homosexuality on her own. Call me a bad friend, if you may, but I felt that I did the right thing. I listened as she replayed what she'd seen. She walked into the house in search of him. Only to find him in the back room being screwed by the guy she'd known the entire time as his best friend and another locally known drug dealer. The fact that she had been in a committed relationship with this man for years and even birthed two of his children was devastating.

Being blinded by his masculine demeanor and financial status, physically and mentally impaired her judgment and left her heartbroken. Ladies, don't be fooled by these physical appearances. Don't walk in and catch your man indulging in homosexuality. Be aware of his sexuality before something drastic happens. This is the only way to prevent yourself from the inevitable heartbreak you'll experience upon finding out about your man and his secret life.

Many men display negativity toward openly gay men; it's not because they dislike them, but only because underneath their hardcore personalities, they're just like them.

"I hate fags!"

"Kill all queers."

"Gays are an abomination."

"Man, that shit is nasty."

"Keep that shit away from me."

"I'm not on that gay shit."

INSECURITY

Whatever the hate may be, whatever the slurs may indicate, if a man is constantly expressing how he feels about another man's sexual preference, then that's a clear indication he's gay. He displays these negative reactions because he's insecure about his sexuality; so instead of admiring an openly gay guy, he displays hate.

When I was younger, I couldn't understand why so many guys hated me. I had to daily fight the bullies that called me names and declared war against me for being openly gay. Being young, I didn't understand the nature of a man; nonetheless, one that was undercover. It wasn't until I started dating and preferring more masculine men that I realized the negative reactions were just a feign. Dealing with those certain types of men, helped me develop a better understanding of their actions toward other gay men. In all actuality, it was their way of gaining attention or making discreet advances. A man, who's one hundred percent straight, will never have an issue or be insecure when a gay man is present. In fact, it won't bother him at all if he's completely secure with himself and his sexuality.

I remember relaying this information to my sister, who laughed in my face! That was until we were in the nightclub, and this guy approached us at the bar. At first, I didn't recognize him due to the dark lighting in the club. He was obviously in his down low mode because my sister was his choice. He flashed his smile and engaged in small talk with her. She hadn't dismissed him, so I assumed she was intrigued by his tall frame and dark, handsome features. I nearly choked on the contents of my drink once I finally realized who he was. I'd just had sex with this guy the prior week. It was nothing serious, just a fling with a hot guy from social media. But the fact that he was now trying to hook up with my sister bothered me.

When he finally recognized me, due to the fact I purposely made it obvious, he immediately turned defensive from thinking I would expose him. He exchanged numbers with my sister and briskly walked away. I was furious!

Disgusted with the entire situation, I turned to her and told her to delete his number immediately. Being a female, a naïve one, who was obviously clueless about the world of down low and undercover men, she wanted to know why? I felt sorry for her as I do for all females who are being deceived and manipulated by these undercover men. I had to spare her feelings by hurting her feelings. "He's gay," I said.

Thinking I was on one of my all men are gay rants, she laughed, and took a sip of her drink. I took that as a sign she didn't believe me. So I pulled out my phone, searched my contacts, and highlighted his number. Still dreading the fact that I was raining on her parade, I turned the phone in her direction so she could see the name and number were the same ones he'd just given her. The look on her face displayed her disappointment.

This is one of the many reasons I decided to write this book. A lot of women are tricked and blindsided by the men they chose to deal with. Had I not been present at that nightclub, this guy would have probably ended up not only sleeping with me but screwing my sister as well.

Since the nightclub incident, my sister hasn't dated a guy without first bringing him to meet her gay brother.

Part of that is to make sure I haven't slept with them, which is fine with me; but its more for observation. She never reveals to them that her brother is gay and flamboyant. By the time they realize the obvious, the observation has begun. If he's undercover, he'll be caught off guard. His insecurities will flare up and reveal his true identity. We call this "The Test."

If you want to run the test on your man, or a man you intend on dating, set the stage or chose the right occasion, and run the test. Invite your most flamboyant friend or friends over and allow them to do the most while observing your man. If he's undercover and insecure, he'll immediately try to remove himself from the room. Fear of being clocked will have him completely on edge. If he stays and shows no sign than their liveliness intimidates him, then he's a keeper. Remember to be attentive during the test. His actions will reveal all you need to know.

"*If social media accounts are marked private, preventing other's from seeing pictures or posting comments, he's hiding something from you.*"

OPPORTUNITY

Today's society is not divided by a world of gay and straight man. It's based more on opportunity. There are only two categories in which I classify men: gay and curious. Obviously, there are straight men out there somewhere, but the only difference separating the two is a distant circumstantial opportunity.

A straight man's curiosity isn't what makes him gay. Curiosity is what makes him indulge, and indulging is what makes him gay. A lot of straight men have thoughts without ever recognizing they're doing so. For instance, a lot of straight men like to ask, "What would make a man sleep with another man with all the women in the world?"

Even though it's in the form of a question, the fact that he's questioning the motives or intentions of another man displays his curiosity. Some men will leave it at that, but we all know that, "Curiosity always kills the cat!"

Some men will allow curiosity to intrigue them so much; they will decide to gain a broader understanding, so they will be able to relate. To relate, they must participate. Believe it or not, ladies, it's happening.

If you're in a committed relationship with a man who may be indulging, it will be hard for him to navigate around you. For him to act on his curiosity, he must find a discreet opportunity to explore his true sexuality. He has to formulate or devise a plan to conceal his intentions and prevent you and others from knowing. Finding that opportunity can come in many different ways. The most common opportunity is during incarceration. Although he may not be planning a trip to the big house anytime soon, prison is the type of setting or environment where homosexuality runs wild. It's almost considered normal. Prison is not the only place a man can find the opportunity to indulge. Homosexuality in society is just as relevant. A man's whole objective is to do it discreetly no matter the setting or environment.

Another place an opportunity can present itself is online. Social media is the biggest breeding ground for discreet hookups. Then there are thousands of gay websites, which makes it easy to indulge, on top of all the 1-800 numbers available for chatting online. Add that to the number of streets within your city limits that are known for prostitution and solicitation from both men and women, and you have yourself a broad window of opportunities to select from.

Whichever way he decides to go about engaging in the opportunity to explore his homosexuality, you'll be unaware of his participation. You have to be attentive, ladies; paying attention to his body language and behavior is crucial during your detection period. His movements, slang, and flamboyant behavior will be on display, but if you're not paying absolute attention, you'll miss it every time – if you don't have a trained eye. Only after he's taken advantage of the opportunity and exposed himself to homosexuality will he start to display certain characteristics and signs that you can pick up on. Being able to distinguish if he's curious or not can be difficult; it's possible but rare. Just continue to be attentive, and he will eventually start to reveal himself without even realizing he's being clocked.

"You can't be aware of his dealings at all times, especially if he's away for years at a time. When he's doing time, you'll be out of sight and certainly out of mind."

PRISON

Doing time is a phrase we have grown to know, whether it's you or someone you may know who has done a jail stint, bid, or prison sentence. Being locked up or locked down has a way of causing change in anyone. That change solely depends on that person and his or her circumstances.

Prison is a place where criminals are confined and can freely be who they want to be, without answering to anyone. Families are hundreds of miles away. The men around don't really exist because at the EOS, end of their sentences, they will never be seen or heard from again. Basically, it's a world of freedom, freedom to do whatever the fuck they want. It's similar to that of a menagerie.

I will be honest with you; I won't sugarcoat anything. If I'm telling you something, it's real. It's not statistics or research, scientific study or observation. It's not what I think; it's what I know. Prison will change a man mentally, physically, and sexually. Not all men will experience this change, but those who may have been living their lives as a closet case in society will experience some changes. I won't go into much detail about my personal prison experiences because this isn't about me; it's about revealing the true identity of your man.

But I will say that I have experienced the prison life and all that it has to offer. From detention centers to state institutions, two things never change: The nasty ass food and the lust. The need for sexual attention is at an all-time high. When a man is behind bars, his nature is in overdrive. A guy, who's used to having sex every day or even three or four times a week, won't last very long after being stripped and deprived of his sexual nature. Some men have strong willpower and remain strong; others are not that fortunate.

First, a man will try self-pleasing strategies to remain celibate. Only the strong and a truly straight man survives this stage. Masturbating, also referred to as jacking or jerking off, is a temporary relief and less than ten times as satisfying as actual human contact. So, his sex drive will remain in overdrive while he fights within himself to save his sexuality.

Truth is, nearly ninety percent of the prison population is indulging in homosexuality, whether openly or secretly indulging. Prison is a place, where men are given discreet opportunities to explore their sexualities. A lot of things are overlooked or accepted based on the nature and circumstances of the situation, homosexuality being at the top of that list.

There are a lot of different reasons men decide to indulge or participate in homosexuality while incarcerated. The sexual pleasure is just one of many reasons men indulge. The opportunity presents itself, and they take it. As long as they continue to display masculine roles, the other straight men will respect them enough to consider them straight. This is how they cope with or embrace being gay in prison.

Another common reason is financial gain. A lot of men who are doing time, go through a certain period in prison they refer to as "hard times." You may have seen that tattoo a few times. Hard times is in reference to their families not being financially stable enough to accommodate their stay in prison, thus leaving them in a very uncomfortable environment.

Choosing an openly gay guy also referred to as a "boy" or "baby" to befriend would be a means of survival.

These particular types of guys start off by just using the "boys" or "babies" for money and other material assets but, after a short period, his actions go from surviving to indulging. Then there's the group of guys who indulge out of curiosity. However this may occur, it's easy for a man to participate in homosexuality in a prison setting without consequences or repercussions. There's absolutely no way for you to know exactly what took place during his incarceration, and unfortunately, the rules in prison are just as they are in Las Vegas: Whatever happens there; stays there.

Once these men are released from prison and back in society, they will return to women, portraying to be straight men, blinding you with their rock-hard bodies, bad boy tattoos, and thuggish demeanors. True enough, what girl doesn't want a bad boy? But the real question at hand is what woman wants another man's boy? I mean, seriously, are you ready to deal with the consequences of sleeping with a man who has been intimate with another man? Are you ready to take the risk of contracting something incurable from a man who's been having unprotected sex in an unprotected environment with another man? Can you deal with the possibility of him continuing to sleep with other men after being released from jail or prison? Ladies, these are the things you must consider before committing to a man who has a history of doing or serving time.

If your man is currently serving a sentence, you should be very concerned. After living a homosexual lifestyle behind bars, he will return home, and you will be his preference.

"Physical, mental, and verbal abuse can stem from uncontrollable emotions. In these types of situations, women usually become victims due to their men's infidelities."

BATTLING THE URGE

A lot of men can't cope or deal with the circumstances of life or accept the decisions they may have made. I'll break this down, so you're on the same page. A man who can't cope or deal with the circumstances of life, simply means whatever cards life may have dealt him whether gay, straight, bisexual, rich, poor, black, or white—if he feels life should be different, then he'll develop physical, mental, and emotional issues. Some may even result in committing suicide. Not being able to deal with a certain decision means he's regretful or ashamed of the choices he has made.

When a man realizes he's gay, or once he decides to indulge in that lifestyle, two things will happen: He's going to seek that thrill to the greatest extent because it's new and exciting. The other is, he'll try to hide it because of the fear factor. Fear of rejection and afraid of what others will think.

This is when he'll try to suppress the feelings toward other men, and the battle of the urge begins.

Now I've spoken on the life of a prisoner, what doing time consists of, and the effects it can have on a man mentally, physically, and sexually. Once he's released from jail or prison, that's when the real battle begins. I have a relative who's in love with a handsome, sexy, masculine guy. She's completely head over hills for this guy and would accept him right or wrong, with or without flaws. They have a small child together and, at some point during her pregnancy, he had to go to prison to serve a short sentence. Before he went off to prison, their relationship was a healthy one. She visited him often, had the baby, and continued her support while he was incarcerated.

Once he was released, things seemed normal for a while. But after some time, that urge came, his sexual frustrations surfaced. He started to beat her repeatedly for no reason, finding reasons to fuss and fight, so he could stay away for days and sometimes weeks at a time. After satisfying his sexual desires, he'd return with the obvious gifts and apologies. Being a female, she didn't see the signs, wasn't catching the clues that spoke volumes that something about her man was different. Of course, the first thing she thought was he had developed some mental issue from serving time in prison. For some undisclosed reason, she thought prison had a way of making men insane.

Truth is, he wasn't insane; he was gay. Prison is not like the wars, where you develop post-traumatic stress disorder also known as (PTSD). That's for veterans, not prisoners. Prison is a lot of things, and it does affect one's transition back into society. But it doesn't make a man violent or hateful toward those who supported him during his time of incarceration.

She was clueless for quite some time until things started to reveal themselves. It turned out that he had been having sex with other men while in prison. Once released, he didn't have that unlimited selection at his disposal. He couldn't cover up his homosexuality with the rules of how prison operates. Society was different and wouldn't overlook his sexuality no matter what position he played. He beat her because his appetite for men was raving. She was no longer what he craved, no longer what he wanted, and no longer fulfilled his desires. He blamed her for his weakness, his sentence, and his decisions.

Ladies, you need to understand that when you're dealing with a man who's on the down low, you're just his puppet. His prop that he carries around to make a statement. You're the person who continues to make everybody think he's straight, so he keeps you around for that purpose. He's not in love with you, and he doesn't want you. The sex may be great for you; but in his mind, he's giving a little to get a lot. The minute you start to notice certain things, he'll turn aggressive to show masculinity, by abusing you verbally, mentally, and physically.

A lot of women frequently experience domestic violence. A lot of that violence can stem from drug and alcohol abuse, childhood issues, or many other things. Don't exclude the possibility that he's violent because he's living two different lifestyles.

Be mindful of these characteristics and signs. Don't become a victim of domestic violence or any abuse because of the decision he's made, or the skeletons he's fighting. Just because he's trapped in the closet doesn't mean you need to be in the closet with him. Get out and get help immediately.

A man can also be battling the urge in many other ways aside from abusing you. There's also self-abuse. That can be the constant use of drugs and alcohol. His normal demeanor may become saddened or depressed, and his physical appearance may also reflect a battle disregarding his hygiene or grooming. Battling the urge is one of the hardest parts of living on both sides of the fence, but it can lead to the ultimate revelation of a man's homosexuality.

WEAKLING

I want to set the record straight on who's strong, and who's weak. Naturally, when we think of a man, we think of strength. When I say weakling, I'm not referring to physical strength, but mental and moral strength. The strength of men is solidified by high positions of power and kings of castles. I'm not saying they don't deserve those titles or positions; I'm simply imposing it doesn't prevent them from being weak or having a weakness.

There's an old saying, "Behind every successful man is a strong woman." That, ladies, is a true statement. So why it is that women are not given the proper amount of recognition? Although women's mental and moral strengths are what completes his overall physical strength, they're still referred to as the weak link. I don't agree with that at all. There are too many strong women to consider any of them weak.

My mother was Superwoman! She worked two jobs and single-handedly raised eight children, three of her own and five foster. Somehow, she provided us with all the essentials to live happily under one roof. We had everything we needed and some of what we wanted, attended cheerleading practice, football games, after-school programs, music recitals, and even court dates for those of us who just couldn't keep our asses out of trouble! Cooking, cleaning, and family time was also in the midst, all without the help of a man. Let's see a man demonstrate that type of strength.

There are so many wives, mothers, grandmothers, and aunts who are superwomen but never get the recognition they deserve. The Bible says, "Woman was created from the rib of man." If that is true, then she was created from his strongest rib.

Never let the actions or decisions of a man make you feel that you are the weakling.

When God created man, He created him with a weakness. God created man with a penis, forever branding him a weakling. It's obvious that a man's penis controls about 90 percent of his decision-making abilities. Once he's erect, all of his rational thinking and better judgment is out the window, thus making him a weakling: relating to or acting on the mind, character, or will. Take it from a man, ladies, being rational is extremely difficult when you have a hard-on.

The Bible describes the weakness of a man, during the history of creation. A lot of people are going to disagree with what I have to say, but it's my fucking opinion, and I'm no weakling. We all know the biblical story of Adam and Eve.

Although there are many different versions and descriptions of this story, the facts are the same.

Genesis 2:8 *And the Lord planted a garden eastward in Eden, and there is where he put man in whom he had formed.*

Remember, ladies, **Genesis 2:7** *said, "God created man from the dust of the ground."* So, just from that verse alone, you should know that man was created weak. Dust is a finely powdered matter; a particle that can be easily wiped or blown away. Nothing about dust represents strength.

Genesis 2:9 *And out of the ground the Lord God made every tree grow that is pleasant to the sight and good for food. The tree of life was also in the midst of the garden, and the tree of knowledge of good and evil.*

Genesis 2:15 *says, "And God took man and put him in the Garden of Eden to tend to it and keep it."* Meaning God wanted Adam dust-made ass to do a little yard work.

Genesis 2:16 *And the Lord God commanded the man, saying, "Of every tree in this garden, you may freely eat; but of the tree of knowledge of good and evil, you shall not eat, for the day that you eat of it, you shall surely die."* God was speaking not of physical death, ladies, but spiritual death.

Genesis 2:18 *And the Lord God said, "It is not good that man should be alone; I will make him a helper comparable to him."*

Genesis 2:19 *Out of the dust* [Again, God created man some dusty ass friends]. *God formed every beast of the field and every bird of the air and brought them to Adam to see what he would call them. Whatever Adam called each living creature, that was its name.* So, Adam named all the cattle, all the birds of the air, and every beast of the field.

After giving Adam all these things, he was still weak. He still cried that none of the living creatures, created of the same dust in which he was created, were comparable to him to be his helper. By this time, God was sick of all of Adam's crying. God knew that man was weak and couldn't manage alone. So, he gave him something stronger, something wiser, and something greater. He gave him woman; and that, ladies, is when you were created. Not from dust like Adam and his beastly friends, but from bone of bone and flesh of flesh. Bones are hard and not easily broken; flesh is tough and not easily torn. Ladies, you represent strength.

Genesis 2:21 *And the Lord God caused a deep sleep to fall on Adam, and he slept; and He took his rib and closed up the flesh in its place. Then the rib, which the Lord God had taken from Adam, He made into a woman and brought her to him.*

Genesis 2:25 *And they were both naked, Adam and Eve; and they were not ashamed.*

So, Adam awakened from his deep sleep, and Eve was there, Naked! Immediately temptation was present, but since the Bible is man wrote, man will never admit that he was the first to be tested and men are the real reason sin was introduced into the world. This was when the blame was put on the woman to indicate that she was the weakling.

Genesis 3 *Now the serpent was more cunning than any beast of the field, which the Lord God created. And he said* *to Eve, "Has God indeed said, you shall not eat from the tree of the garden?"*

And Eve said to the serpent, "We may eat the fruit of the trees of the garden. But of the fruit of the tree which is in the midst of the garden. God has said, You shall not eat it, nor touch it, lest you die."

The serpent said to Eve, "You will not surely die, for God knows that in the day you eat of it, your eyes will be opened, and you will be like God, knowing good and evil."

So, Eve ate from the tree, and the sight was pleasant to her eyes, so she took a piece of fruit to Adam, and he ate, and his sight was pleasant, too.

When God walked into the garden, **Genesis 3:10** *says, Adam hid behind a bush.* Now **Genesis 2:25** already told you that Adam and Eve were naked, and they knew it and wasn't ashamed. *So, after God saw that Adam was hiding, he called out to him, saying, "Why are you hiding?"*

Adam said, "Because I'm naked." God knew this was untrue because he had been naked all the while. Truth was, Adam was aroused! He had an erection and was ready to become sexually active.

Man wants you to believe that the serpent had tricked Eve; and then, she deceived Adam. When all along, Adam was already fighting temptation. He was already formulating a plan to get laid without God knowing. He wanted Eve as soon as he awakened from his sleep and saw her naked body. God had put the temptation of flesh right before his eyes because he knew Adam was weak. He tested Adam way before the serpent tried deceiving Eve, and Adam failed miserably.

Instead of Adam just being honest when God questioned him about his hiding, he did exactly what men do today. He lied.

Genesis 3:12 *Then Adam said, "The woman whom you gave to be with me, she gave me of the tree, and I ate."*

That pissed me off because not only was Adam weak, he was also a liar and a snitch. He threw Eve under the bus, not taking any responsibility for having a hard dick in the middle of the Garden of Eden. God should have hauled off and slapped the living shit out of him for being so fucking weak. God had given him all these many things, and all of the earth including common sense. Adam knew right from wrong, but because he thought God wouldn't find out, and opportunity presented itself, he said fuck it. He couldn't resist the temptation of getting laid, thus making him a weakling.

This man-written Scripture wants you to think that women were weak before men. It wants you to think that a snake convinced Eve to deceive Adam, and woman was the reason sin was introduced into the world. Men refused to take responsibility for their actions. Adam allowed his sexual nature to cloud his judgment exactly how men allow it to happen today. They don't just slip and fall into the vagina of another woman or the ass of some man; their weakness is sex. They were not created from rock, brick, or stone; they were created from dust! So, the first opportunity he gets to be laid, he'll take it. No matter what the opposing gender is. Physically, he's bigger and stronger; mentally and morally, he's weaker.

The minute he's locked in a jail or prison cell and can't get the sexual satisfaction of a woman, he'll sacrifice and substitute you for another man without thinking twice. Weakling! The minute his curiosity soars through the roof, and he can no longer contain himself, he'll seek the opportunity to explore his sexual desires full throttle.

Weakling! When he's another man's bitch, instead of loving and cherishing you, he becomes envious of you; then beats you to prove he's a man. He's so uncomfortable and unsure of himself; he immediately becomes defensive and displays negative behavior to mask his identity out of fear of being recognized as one of their own. Weakling!

However you decide to look at the situation, the fact remains the same: men have a weakness, and it's that thing between their legs. Don't let his weaknesses continue to go unseen. You're smarter and stronger; you're a thinker, and he's a weakling!

"When it's revealed, women, who are in denial about their men being gay, will experience the worst type of heartbreak."

THE UGLY TRUTH

Although women are not directly the blame for the choices or sexual desires of undercover men, some women are responsible for condoning them. I understand that there is a shortage of men. I really do get it, but that should not justify homosexuality being brought into your home. To settle for a piece of man, rather than having no man at all displays a weakness. That weakness is what allows a man room to explore his sexuality and make excuses for his behavior. He knows you will not leave him because you have displayed that your weakness is loneliness. So, he will use that against you, putting you at a disadvantage to continue being deceived.

For some reason, no one wants to be alone; but what woman wants to be sexually and emotionally involved with a man who's sexually or emotionally involved with another man? For God's sake, it's hard enough trying to keep them from sleeping with other women and harder to accept sharing them with another man. It's sad to say; but the ugly truth is, there are a lot of women who are accepting homosexuality to keep these men. These women think they can reform these men.

Truth is, he'll never change. Once he's gay, he's gay for the stay. He will find a way to convince you that he's no longer participating or indulging in the lifestyle but still do it behind your back.

What bothers me is that after all the bullshit women have endured, the fights and hardships they have had to overcome for equality, they should empower one another, lift each other up. They shouldn't degrade themselves or lower their standards for the sake of keeping a man, especially a gay one.

What about your daughters, nieces, and sisters? The younger women who look to you for guidance or those who consider you a role model. What type of message are you sending when you're saying that it is okay to sleep with a man who's homosexual? I won't sugarcoat this or dress it up to make it sound pretty. The women who are lowering their standards and subjecting themselves to this type of bullshit are pathetic with low self-esteem.

The ugly truth is, not only are men responsible for the declining number of one hundred percent straight men, but the women who are accepting and contributing to their homosexuality are just as responsible. Women are also making it hard for other women to find and keep a straight man. Why would he be with a woman who wants him straight when he can have one who will accept him any way he comes.

As I've said before, if I'm relaying information to you or giving insight into a certain situation, it's because I've lived and experienced it. Not long ago. I experienced a bad breakup. It's still painful for me to talk about, but I want all women to know the shit I'm telling you is real. The words you're reading are not of my mind but from my heart.

I was in a relationship with a guy, who I swore I was going to spend the rest of my life with. In my eyes, he was the definition of perfection. We were together five years. After the first year, he proposed to me. Before he and I started dating, he had only dated females. So, I was his first homosexual experience and relationship (so he said).

For five long years, I took care of him while he was in prison, tended to his every need, even financially supported his family in his absence. He promised me the moon and the stars above. I believed him because I loved, adored, and cherished this man.

Once he was released from prison, he betrayed me. Robbed me of thousands of dollars and got re-engaged to a female. His sorry excuse to me was that even after living a homosexual lifestyle in prison for five years, he couldn't see himself living openly gay in society. With the thousands of dollars that he took from me, he went and started a new life, moved to a discreet location, made his social media accounts private, and changed his phone number. All in the attempt to keep his new fiancé blind and clueless.

When I heard the news of the engagement, I was devastated. I went to work trying to locate this bastard. I had to warn this woman about the man she was about to marry. I wanted to let her know that the image in front of her eyes was an illusion, a misleading appearance.

I eventually found out her name, located her through social media and informed her of the soon-to-be husband's real sexual preference. I sent her pictures, letters, and emails of our five-year relationship to ensure her that he was who I proclaimed him to be. Guess what she did?

Lowered her standards if she ever had any to begin with, degraded herself, and married the son of a bitch. That was extremely shocking to me because she has children, including young boys. Not only did she subject herself to the possibility of being hurt in the future from homosexual infidelity, but she also put the safety and innocence of her children at risk of being exposed to that lifestyle.

This woman, along with many other women, are the one's responsible for the pain and despair of many good women in search of a decent straight man. Don't let the insecurity of these pathetic women be the reason you end up sleeping with, dating, or marrying an undercover man. Certainly, don't be a woman who's destroying the lives of other women by accepting it. Enough men are indulging, lying, and hiding their sexuality to carry that burden themselves. It's better to lose someone you feel is a winner than to walk away a loser.

"Men don't possess the same willpower as women to adhere to abstinence, regardless of the opposing gender. If a discreet circumstance presents itself, he'll surrender to sexual gratification every time."

"Denial is the first stage of distinguishing an undercover man. Even when there's truth, denial will be his shield."

CONFESSIONS OF UNDERCOVER MEN

*O*n more than one occasion, I've asked myself what exactly caused me to indulge in an alternative lifestyle. But unlike most men, I've never been molested or sexually abused. So that eliminates a long list of possible traumatic events, which could have triggered my perversion of a submissive bottom. Today, I will attempt to bring you into my world; a world where few men will admit to, but many indulge in.

Being a child of the 80s, indulging in homosexual activity was considered taboo. As times changed, so did society views on homosexuality. Today, it's not only socially acceptable behavior; it's often promoted everywhere I look. So as time blew past, I went from being a homophobic "fag-basher" to a curious Black man. And by me being from the Black Mecca of the south, where not only homosexuality but black homosexuality runs wild, it *was easy to relax on my stance against homosexuality. My first sexual experience came late, by most people's standards. But it occurred in a place where homosexuality was an everyday part of life. I was nineteen and in prison. Out of curiosity, I allowed a boy to suck me off. Immediately after he swallowed every drop of me, I felt conflicted.*

On one hand, I felt disgusted like, "Did I just do that?" But on the other hand, I realized besides the fact that this was another man who had just sucked me off, taken every inch, and swallowed every drop I pumped out, there wasn't much difference between what the women I knew had given me and what I'd just experienced. Actually, it was better in a lot of ways! I wasn't hooked, but I wasn't turned off either.

That experience was maybe what changed my overall view of homosexuality. I didn't have another sexual experience with another man until I was twenty-nine. Once again, I was in prison, and it was only oral.

Even during that time, I never felt like I was gay because I still loved women. I felt I could control my urges and keep that side of me in check, which I've done for the most part. I didn't feel "gay" because unlike most who indulged in homosexuality, I never caught feelings for another man, nor have I crossed that line and anally penetrated another man. So no, in my eyes, I wasn't gay. Curious, maybe. Gay? No. I've had one sexual encounter that led to me catching feelings, or at least the beginning stages of feelings, but it's been a serious struggle to keep those urges and feelings in check because that's something reserved for somebody special! (You know who you are!)

I've done some serious soul-searching, while trying to sort out my stance and feelings toward my new-found perversion for a submissive bottom. From watching other gay couples, I discovered that the love appears to be purer, more passionate than the typical heterosexual relationship. I must admit; I've always been more attracted to the discreet bottoms more than the flamboyant queens. For whatever reason, as of right now, I keep my lifestyle under wraps and live a normal life. My urges aren't a factor at home, work, or anywhere else except in prison if truth be told. But this is my admission, so take it or leave it; I am who I am.

No Name
Atlanta, GA

* * *

I'm a 34-year-old, African American man. I've been incarcerated for six years on a 10-year sentence. I'm also married with four children, and my family means everything to me. Some guys indulge in homosexuality in prison for many reasons such as money, drugs, and sex. I indulged for love. I guess I chose to love the wrong person because it's costing me my life.

We were two guys, who frequented the law library together, trying to find any loopholes or mistakes in our cases that would somehow get us home to our families sooner than the sentence the judge had imposed. We became familiar with each other through our day to day passing and bonded quickly being that we were both dedicated to the same cause, freedom. We started working out together, eating our meals together, even praising and worshipping together. We kept each other balanced.

One day, he confessed his love for me while we were going over a few cases in the law library. His confession completely caught me off guard and angered me. I felt like I'd been manipulated into believing he was trying to get home to his family. All the while, he intended to turn me out. I couldn't stand to be around him another minute, without losing my temper, so I grabbed my shit and hit the door. I just couldn't wrap my mind around the thought that he was gay. His demeanor was always confident and masculine.

I intentionally stayed away from him for a few days while I mentally sorted things out. I wasn't gay! I had a wife and kids. I loved them, and I was going home to them. On the other hand, he was my friend. The only family I had behind the walls. When the phone lines were silenced, lights turned off, and the gates locked, we were cut off from the world beyond our world. It was him I trusted. It was him who keep me sane. I couldn't just turn my back on him; my loyalty wouldn't allow me to disown him because of his sexuality. I eventually had a long talk with him and smoothed things out.

Eventually, I started considering the possibility of experimenting sexually with him; I guess just out of curiosity. I wanted him to know I was with him. I was his friend; I loved him no matter what his sexual preference consisted of.

After two years of sexual intercourse, I was diagnosed with the human immunodeficiency virus (HIV). He had been involved with multiple partners over the years and had never been tested. I had gotten a foot fungus related to athlete's foot and sought medical attention. I was given medication and foot powder that was intended to cure the problem. The fungus wouldn't go away. In fact, it continued to get worse and worse. They eventually ran some tests by taking some blood, and the test results indicated I was HIV positive. I was devastated. At that moment, I knew I'd sacrificed my family and life.

When my wife and children came to visit me, I couldn't even look them in their eyes. The guilt was killing me faster than the virus ever could. When they told me how much they loved me, it broke my heart because I was supposed to love them equally. The choices I made cost me my family and put them at risk. If I can stay out of trouble, I'll be released from prison in the next three years; if I manage to live that long. The medical treatment in prison is limited, so living with a serious illness such as HIV/AIDS can be fatal quickly.

Although I love my family unconditionally, if I could take back the decision I made, I wouldn't because I love him, too. So, I must live with those choices without regret. I hope my family can one day find it in their hearts to forgive me because I don't think I can ever forgive myself.

D. Smith
Orlando, Florida

* * *

I wasn't the richest man in the world or in the streets for that matter, but I hustled hard enough to provide my wife with a good life. She was the reason I risked my freedom every single day. She spent tons of money, wore the best clothing, and drove the finest cars. Taking care of my woman was something I never complained about. It was my responsibility, and I enjoyed every minute of it. My drive to give her the finer things in life is what lead me to prison.

The fact that I was an extremely careful guy in the way I conducted business, ultimately worked in my favor. When the task force finally caught up with me, they only had enough evidence to charge me with felon in possession of a fireman. That single charged cost me five thousand dollars in attorney fees and three years in prison. I left behind everything I owned including house, money, and cars. When I was arrested, she promised me her *love and loyalty. She knew exactly what I expected of her because we had discussed the possibility of my absence many times.*

Things were okay for about the first six months of my sentence. Then things started to change. I guess the saying, "Outta sight, outta mind," is a true statement. She stopped visiting me. I couldn't reach her by phone, and eventually, the letters and money stopped as well. After I had supported her for years, I found myself begging for her support. After all the sacrifices I'd made to ensure her happiness, she was betraying me. It wasn't like I had a lengthy sentence. Three years was a small punishment compared to the huge risk I'd taken in those streets to provide a decent life for her, and a decent life for us. I just couldn't understand her reason for abandoning me.

I finally said, "Fuck it!" and stop trying to be a part of her life. She'd obviously moved on and continued the life I'd given her without me. I started participating in everything prison had to offer. I especially enjoyed gambling. It was the only thing that passed the time and kept my mind off the streets. The guy in charge of the gambling ring was a gay guy. I enjoyed doing business with him because he was a hustler. He reminded me of myself when it came to getting money. He was smart, smooth, and precise. I wasn't one of those guys, who judged people on their appearance or sexual preference. I judge a man by his character. This guy had great characteristics and a lot of ambition.

We became good friends and started hanging out together. Other guys would talk and whisper, but truth be told, I didn't give a fuck! I'd lost the only person whose opinion mattered the most. She'd left me in prison to fend for myself. He and I talked for a few weeks before we started to mess around sexually. I guess you can say I fucked him out of spite from being hurt. My wife had betrayed me, so I was doing everything I could do to remove her from my life.

After my sentence was completed, I kept in touch with him until he was released from prison as well. I'm currently engaged to another woman, but I still see him often. We're good friends if you know what I mean. LOL! Don't blame me; blame my ex-wife.

K.B.
Tampa, Florida

* * *

I can't speak for other men, but I can share my experience on how I became involved in the homosexual lifestyle. Honestly, I used to be one of those guys who was homophobic. I hated anything that was associated with the word gay. That was until I caught a case when I was 17 years old and was sentenced to seven years in prison. I loved tranquility and preferred to have a cell to myself. Unfortunately, in prison, I didn't have a choice. I couldn't choose when I got a cellmate, and I certainly couldn't choose whom that person was.

One day, I got a cellmate. I was furious that my new cellmate was a homosexual. It was a guy who called himself Diamond. I guess he could feel the heat in the room from my temper blazing because he turned to me, and said, "Do you have a problem with me being in this cell?"

I was about to say, "You fucking right! I do! Now get out!" Before I could express my feelings, someone called his name. He turned and exited the room.

I watched him leave; my eyes almost popped out of my head when I saw his ass! This guy had an ass like Buffie the Body. I was mesmerized. In the short period of his absence, I don't know what came over me, but I no longer had an issue with Diamond moving in.

I stuck to my normal routine, going about my daily activities as usual, staying clear of Diamond, and his activities. I also limited all conversation, talking to him as little as possible. To my surprise, he was quiet and respectful! It worked out well for three months. We actually became good friends over time. Diamond changed my outlook on homosexuality, and the way I felt about gay people in general.

This one particular morning, we were locked inside the cell the entire day due to some institutional search drills. Diamond, not wanting to wait until lockdown was over, started to do his morning workout. I swear, he found the smallest pair of shorts he could find to do his squats. He kept his back toward me while he knocked out set after set. I was pretending to be reading a magazine, all the while watching him do his squats. I wondered if those things were the reason his ass was so big. I turned my head away, wondering why I was lusting over another guy. "You're not gay," I told myself.

Later that night, my blood was still boiling from the vision of him doing those squats. He must have felt my demeanor had changed because he asked if there was something on my mind.

I figured I might as well be honest since I was already entertaining the thoughts of possibly indulging. I told Diamond the images of him in those small shorts doing those squats had been on my mind all day. Next thing I knew, I was getting head until I couldn't take it anymore.

Afterward, I didn't know how to feel because physically, it felt good; but emotionally, it felt wrong. *I wasn't gay!* *That feeling quickly went away because almost every night after that, we were sexing each other non-stop.*

So if you want to know if your man is gay, take females out of the equation and replace them with Diamonds.

Megatron
Jacksonville, Florida

* * *

*T*here are a few openly gay people in my family. I guess seeing my family indulging had me open to exploring my sexuality. It first happened when I was about 13 years old. I stayed over a friend's house to attend church the next morning. I assumed he was trying to discover his sexuality just as I was; we ended up fooling around with each other with no clue as to what we were doing. I kept it a secret for years, never wanting my parents to find out that I was attracted to other guys.

From that point on, I dated females and never really felt as if I were gay while trying to keep a grip on my attraction to other men. When I turned 18 years old, I felt that I was an adult; I could do as I pleased. I tried being in a relationship with another man, Of course, it was in secret; but that ended just as quickly as it started due to the fact I was afraid to let him touch me sexually. It was more of a mental and *emotional relationship for me instead of a sexual one. Mentally and emotionally, I was attracted to men. Sexually, I was still attracted to women. I was fighting a hard battle.*

Then like a lot of men, I ended up in prison. That's where I finally got the opportunity to explore and experience the sexual part of the lifestyle. Being that I was already mentally and emotionally involved, it changed me for good. I'm 100 percent committed to being gay. It's been nine years since I've been intimate with a woman, and I'm content with that. I don't have any intentions of hiding who I am or what I am from the world or the women who live in it. I'm happy with the lifestyle I'm currently living.

Dubuy
Largo, Florida

* * *

I had lived in the streets since my mother died in 1996. I was 10 years old and lost with no father figure. All my siblings were older and living lives of their own. I was forced to grow up fast. Dropping out of school and turning to the streets was all I knew to do for means of survival. Fending for myself caused me to experience quite a few things at a young age, but homosexuality wasn't one of them. I was busy trying to make a name for myself, selling drugs, and fucking as many females as possible. I never needed to question my sexuality. I was straight! I mean, I never had a problem with homosexuals; it just wasn't my thing.

Being in the streets, I had to learn how to deal with all kinds of people; so I never developed a complex. I loved beautiful women with big booties. The most beautiful thing God had created. I ended up catching a case when I was 21 years old and was sentenced to almost nine *years in prison. Prison was a different world. The rules and the environment reflected nothing of society.*

After being down for four years, I was standing strong. I had never thought about being sexually involved with another man. One reason was that I was fucking one of the female guards, and the other was because I'd become affiliated with a gang and homosexuality was forbidden. Participating was the fastest way to get shanked or cut across the face, branding one a homosexual for life. After a while I started craving what that had. Within the gang/organization, I had brotherhood; but it consisted of more hate and violence than anything else. The gay relationships I saw consisted more of love and companionship, and that's what I wanted. I'd been away from home for years. It seemed that when I got locked up, the world continued without me. All of my women and friends went on with life without me, and I was lonely.

I started to ask some of the other guys about their experiences in that lifestyle. They all said the same thing, "It's crazy, man; but it's amazing." With about five years left on my sentence, I sat on my bunk and thought about my situation. I was 25 years old, in prison, and seriously considering becoming sexual with another man. I would be risking everything including my life because if my gang brothers found out, they would try to kill me. That meant risking my family, which wasn't a lot to lose since they were nonexistent anyway and risking the loss of my girl. But life had consumed her, and she'd stopped writing after my first two years in prison. The officer I was fucking inside was just pussy and a way to get the things the institution considered contraband, like weed and cigarettes.

After a full night of wrecking my brain, I decided I was going to try it. I was interested in this one guy, but it seemed as if he didn't see me. So, I waited. As time passed, God finally brought us together and OMG it was beautiful. Some men say they found the women of their dreams, but I say I found the man of mine. I'm at the end of my sentence, and we have been together five years. It's been a rollercoaster; but hands down, the best thing that has ever happened to me. The world is ours.

H. Monroe
Orlando, Florida

* * *

I wouldn't consider myself as gay, but I have let a guy suck me off once. I didn't have a girlfriend at the time, so I wasn't cheating or doing anything sneaky. It was late at night. I couldn't find any pussy to get in, so I hopped on the local chat line just to talk to a couple of females to try to land a late-night booty call. There were a few chicks online talking real good, but there was only one who was actually in my area. We connected live and talked for a while before I gave her my direct number.

Women talked for free, but men callers only got a 30-minute free trial period; so giving her my number was a must. Normally, it was fat or straight up ugly chicks on the chat lines. I was horny as hell, so I couldn't be picky. She had a nice voice. She was local, which was convenient and good enough for me. We hung up, and she called me directly. The first thing I noticed was the call came through *as private. So, I thought this chick had to be mad ugly. So, I asked her to describe herself. Of course, she made it seem like she was Beyonce. I laughed, knowing her description would not reflect what she actually looked like. We went back and forth for a while; then I finally asked for the address. I could sense the hesitation, so I decided to speak my fucking mind. "Listen, what the fuck are you stalling for? I don't give a fuck if you look like Beyonce or Celie from The Color Purple."*

I was trying to fuck something. Silence filled the line, and then the truth came. "It's not that; it's just I was born a man," she said.

Now it was my turn to be silent. My first instinct was to hang up on this dude. Then I figured she, he, or whatever had already wasted enough of my time. So what the hell? It was three o'clock in the morning, so nobody would know. On top of that, the voice on the other end of the phone was convincing, I just had to see what was really on the other side of the phone.

After assuring him I wouldn't do anything to jeopardize his safety, he gave me the address. I pulled up. At first glance, what I saw was a female. Even once inside the car, it was still hard to tell. I had come that far, so I was committed. I unzipped my pants, pulled them down, and let the seat back. "Handle your business," ' I said, and he obliged. That was my first and only time I've been intimate with another guy. I love women. I currently have a girlfriend, and I'm happy. I've never stepped out on her with another female and most certainly not with another man. I can't be categorized or labeled as being gay or undercover. Getting head one time doesn't classify me as homosexual. I'm a straight man; I just slipped up one time. Simple as that.

D.J.
Dallas, Texas

* * *

I'm 28 years old, and I've been I guess what they call bi-sexual for a long time. Yes, I've been to prison; however, my indulging came way before my prison sentence ever existed. I slept with a few guys in prison, but I've been intimately involved with men and women for years. It was my best friend who introduced me to that lifestyle. One night, my girl and I got into a heated argument. I left the house just to clear my head. I called up my best friend, and we hit the town.

First, we went to the liquor store; then the strip club. I don't even remember how many drinks I had or how many blunts we smoked. It just felt good to be out of the house and having a good time. The lap dance I was receiving had me at attention; I was in overdrive. By the time we left the club, I could barely walk. My friend decided to drive since I was too intoxicated to do so.

While we drove through the city streets, his hand found my thigh. I wanted to slap his hand away, but the weed and alcohol had me eager. He rubbed my thigh for a few minutes before reaching for my dick. I jumped just off reflex, but his touch relaxed me. Even under the influence, the guilt built up in my stomach. It felt like I had to vomit. He must have felt my reluctance because he slowly removed his hand.

We pulled into a gas station, and he exited the car. Once he was gone, I opened the car door to get some air. Thoughts of my girl filled my head. The guilt had knots in my stomach the size of golf balls. Although my girl and I were constantly on some beef shit, I loved her unconditionally. It just seemed like we couldn't get it right. Even with the vivid thoughts of her in my mind, the stiffness in my jeans wouldn't go down. Blame it on the lap dance or the liquor, whatever the case, I was up and wasn't coming down.

I closed the door and laid back in the seat. A few moments later, he returned and handed me a bottle of water through the passenger window. He pumped the gas, and we drove away. "How long have you been like this?" I asked as we drove in silence.

"Since high school," he answered.

"Damn, man; we've been cool for years, and I never would have known."

"Yeah, I know," he said, "but I'm really sorry for trying to pull you into my world."

I was still fucked up. I surely wasn't going back home to continue arguing with my girl. So, I ended up crashing at his place. I guess between him wanting me, and my hard dick fueled by intoxication, I ended up in his mouth, getting the best head of my life. I've been hooked ever since. I went home the next morning and apologized to my girl. I knew she thought my apology was for the argument the previous night, but it was really for my newly found sexual desire.

Life went on as normal in her eyes. But for me, everything had changed. Yes, I love pussy, but getting sucked off by my best friend every day was something I also loved. The actual sex and penetrating another man didn't come until I went to prison; but by, then I'd already been living undercover for years. I could never see myself being openly gay, so undercover is what I will always be. I'm all in, no turning back now.

Black Boy
Miami, Florida

* * *

I'm a 37 years old Jamaican man, who has been homophobic my entire life. Still is, in a sense. I've always had irrational fear toward gay men, period. I'd always been this way until I was sentenced to 25 years in prison. Growing up in my country, homosexuality was forbidden. I remember seeing men beaten or shot to death for openly stating they were gay, or for even displaying that behavior. So naturally, I grew up to hate homosexuals. I'm still somewhat skeptical about talking to them and uncomfortable being around them. I've been in prison now for 10 years. Although I've been tired a few times, I've been strong enough to keep my dick in my pants.

I've never physically indulged in homo-sexuality, but the homophobic Jamaican is guilty of being curious. I've allowed someone to peek my interest. The majority of the openly gay dudes in prison are outright disrespectful. This one, in *particular, was different. I would see him watching me and instantly become angry, but he never crossed the line. A lot of the other guys respected him for two reasons: he had money, and he wasn't soft. He stood up for himself, which was a big thing in prison. Having heart meant survival. Although all the other guys seemed to like him, I hated him. At least, that's what I thought.*

After a while, I got used to him staring at me or just being in the same vicinity. I went from getting angry to laughing and smirking. This guy found a way to get close to me. Yeah, eventually, the hateful Jamaican and the bati-boi became cool.

Even though cell phones are illegal in prison, it seemed as if everyone owned one. We also shared our numbers with everybody who owned a cell phone in case of an emergency, like an institution shakedown or the possibilities of the guards conducting dormitory searches.

At night when I was done talking to the many females I had on my team, I would text him just to say, "What's up?" We would never flirt openly because I wouldn't allow it, and he knew that. So, we texted each other every night while sleeping three bunks away from each other. It became almost a ritual. Every night after I talked to my chicks, I called and texted my bati boi. His conversation had me hooked. He knew exactly what to say to keep my undivided attention. I especially loved when he talked in his little fake New York accent. That really turned me on.

One night, the conversation got so heated, we ended up having phone sex. But since it wasn't physical, I still consider myself to be straight. I'm just guilty of a little harmless conversation.

Island Boy
West Palm Beach, Florida

* * *

*F*irst and foremost, I can't believe I'm putting this on paper. There's no doubt I'm a straight man. I was sentenced to 15 years in prison. It's where I had my first and only homosexual experience. I was cellmates with this guy, who was in a serious relationship with this "baby," a nickname for all openly gay guys in prison. Well, the feminine ones for that matter.

Prison is based on respect. So as long as my cellmate respected me enough to keep that gay shit out of my face, I respected him enough to give him space to do his thing. I was heavy into the Bible and trying to do the right thing, counting on God to free me mentally and physically. When the "baby" would come to my cell to see my cellmate, I would get up and leave. I never said anything to my cellmate about the comings and goings of his partner. I just wanted to give them their space *because when I wanted a little peace and quiet, I expected the same thing.*

After a while, the "baby" would speak to me and make small conversation. I guess to ease any suspected tension in the air. That's what we called "channel checking" in prison. If I had displayed any sign of negativity from him opening the links of communication, he probably would have stayed away from my cell. Truth be told, I didn't have an issue. I wasn't homophobic; I just wasn't into what they were into.

When he and my cellmate would disagree or have arguments, somehow, I found myself being the sounding board. I'd been in between the two of them quite a few times. This one particular day, they had a bad fight. At the end of the drama, the "baby" was crying. I don't know why, but I was hurt. Seeing him cry did something to me; I wanted to kill my cellmate for hurting him. I was so angry I grabbed my towel and washcloth and left the room immediately. While I was in the shower, I tried to make sense of the reason why I was feeling the way

I was about this guy. Where were these sudden feelings coming from? He wasn't my baby, and I wasn't gay. Yet, I felt obligated to protect him.

When I made it back to the cell, all of the commotions were over, and my cellmate sat alone in the cell. "Man, I'm sorry about all that," he said.

"No problem, man; just try not to hurt him like that again."

"What?"

"I mean if you love him like you say you do and want to keep him." I reasoned knowing I'd said too much.

The look on his face confirmed my thoughts. I had to somehow clear the air. This was my cellmate; and in prison, I couldn't just leave shit hanging in the air and sleep peacefully without consequences.

"Look, man," I said. "I don't fuck around with other men, but I live in this cell with you; so, unfortunately, I have to see and hear everything that happens in here. Not only that but you've told me how you feel about him, so I'm just giving you a little advice, nothing more. So. don't look at me like that."

"Yeah, all right," he said.

From that day forward, I made it my business to let "baby" know I was feeling him. Little hints here and there seemed to work well. He walked into the cell one afternoon, looking for my cellmate. I figure then was the perfect time to make my move. I took off my white t-shirt, revealing my rock-hard body and chiseled abs. I was taunting him. When his eyes fell on my chest and ran down my body, I knew I had him. I walked straight up to him and kissed his lips. I was moving strictly off impulse because I had no experience whatsoever.

"No!" he said, pushing me away. "You're going to get me in trouble."

"Fuck that, nigga; he can't keep hurting you. He can't make you happy." I spoke with pure emotion.

"Oh, and you can?" he asked with attitude.

"Let me show you." I grabbed him by the neck and kissed him softly. This time, he invited me to explore his lips.

After that day, we sexed each other every opportunity we got. The sex was so good that I got his zodiac sign tattooed on me, LOL! I figured his name would be too obvious being that I shared a cell with his man. Call me a dirty dog, but "baby" was my bitch, too. After about a year, I got transferred, and I never saw him again. I have about three years left on my sentence. I'm leaving prison exactly how I came, a straight man. Will I ever sleep with another man once I'm released from prison? That depends on the circumstances and the individual.

For now, my experience is a well-kept secret. I intend on keeping it that way.

Papi Chulo
Orlando, Florida

* * *

I was 16 years old, and my girl was pregnant with my son. My life changed that year. Although I was happy about being a dad, I'd grown tired of just sitting around the house catering to her every need. It wasn't that I didn't enjoy taking care of her, I was young and needed a little free time of my own.

This one particular evening, I decided I was going to hang out. I was driving down the street and saw what I thought was a female, at first glance. When I got closer, I knew I was staring at a guy. Growing up, I was always attracted to other guys; but being so young, I never acted on it. I wasn't into drag queens or cross-dressers. I was attracted more to regular guys like myself. At that moment, I didn't care. It was time I explored my curiosity.

He got in the car, and we went back to his place. I was a nervous wreck. I had only fantasized about being with another guy. I never thought it would happen.

Nothing happened that day; we just talked about life in general. I guess he could sense I was younger than him, and a virgin to the lifestyle. He was very patient and didn't pressure me at all. After about four or five days, I built up enough courage to become intimate with him. The experience was amazing. Something I had never experienced in my young life.

I eventually became overly possessive about him. I found myself neglecting my baby mother and my unborn child. One thing led to another, and the relationship became mentally and physically violent. I was turning into a mad man. I would beat him every chance I got. I was mad at him for making me love him. He finally left me, and I've been lonely ever since.

The feelings I feel when I'm with a man is a completely different feeling than when I'm with a woman. I'm still attracted to women, but I have a strong desire to be with other men. It's just something inside of me that wants to please and be pleased. A female can never do for me what a guy can. The woman I'm committed to will never know it, but she will always share me with a man.

Eventually, my son was born. I was a proud father and very much a part of his life. The mother of my son remains unaware of my sexual encounters or my sexual desires. I plan to keep it that way.

Trillville
Sarasota, Florida

* * *

I was in my first year in college and adjusting well. Football tryouts were approaching, and I was ready to get on the field. Although I loved sports, I'd never participated in high school. I kept my head in the books, which landed me a full academic scholarship. I figured I should loosen up a bit and do something I loved. I tried out and made the team. One day after practice, everybody hit the shower. I was secure with my sexuality and didn't mind showering with a group of guys. I was straight and thought the same of my teammates.

After quickly cleaning up, the guy's piled in the shower and exited one by one. Not having any classes or obligations for the next hour, I decided to shower a little longer. Before I knew it, the shower was empty. I closed my eyes for a few minutes with my head under the water. Once I'd had enough, I shut the water off and toweled off. I *got out and walked around the wall to the locker area. The sight before me made me freeze.*

On the bench behind the wall, stood one of my teammates while the other gave him a blow job. I was in total shock. They noticed me watching and stopped momentarily, long enough to notice my harden penis through the towel. I don't know how my dick had risen. What I did know was that I wanted to take off running, but I was stuck. Gravity wouldn't let me move. The one standing, walked over to me, removed the towel, dropped to his knees, and took me into his mouth. The three of us did things I doubt any of our girlfriends would be happy to hear about.

That was the only time I've been with another guy. I graduated college, got a great job, married a beautiful woman, and was blessed with two awesome children. I haven't indulged in homosexuality since college, but I do think about it all the time. In fact, it's constantly on my mind.

It's a struggle every day to stay faithful to my wife and kids. My wife is clueless about my past experiences and my current desires. Sometimes it's hard to get aroused and please my wife sexually because of my constant urge to be pleased by another guy. Life is good right now; I'm not trying to destroy the lives of my children because of my sexual desires. So, for now, I'll continue to try and overcome my desires and be the best husband and father I can be.

Family Man
Tallahassee, Florida

* * *

I'm 50 years old with a great amount of time remaining on my prison sentence. I grew up in an all-male household with just mom. She was the only female in the house. Naturally, I'm a masculine man since I grew up with only brothers. I tried dating girls but always made a mess of everything. I guess my father and brother had taught me all the wrong things to do. So, going through life without a preference, the only thing a female could do for me was serve me sexually.

Even that wasn't always satisfying. Sometimes I wondered why I was unhappy sexually but never credited that to the possibility that I was gay. Then, like a lot of men, I ended up going to prison and began craving the attention from the feminine "girly" acting inmates.

At first, I thought the attractions were due to their flamboyant ways. I later discovered the attraction was physical, emotional, and mental. It took some time for me to accept the fact that I'm gay. I've used women throughout my life to suppress the real me without even noticing I was doing so. Will I do another female? Maybe, but right now, I'm enjoying my life as a happily gay man.

D. Lake
Fort Lauderdale, Florida

Never say never.

REALITY CHECK

The reality of this situation is that the world is constantly changing. Evolving right before our eyes into something we've never seen. Anything that we once considered as the correct way to live or being normal is long gone.

Even after reading this book, unfortunately, a lot of women will still become victims of a down low man. These men are good at deceiving women, each of them possessing their own unique style, grace, and finesse. Adroit at maneuvering skillfully through life, destroying woman after woman. The deceitful intentions of these men will remain the same.

It's best to know as much as possible about the lifestyle of an undercover man as you can. The more you know, the better off you are at staying clear of a man who's indulging in a homosexual lifestyle. When dealing with any man, everything involving you and your life should be a major factor in the decision you make on committing to him. You have everything to lose. Everything is at stake including your children, your job, and your health. Allowing a man to bring homosexuality into your home and deceive you, can ultimately result in the loss of everything that's most important to you. He tries to keep his lifestyle a secret to prevent the loss of everything that means the most to him, while destroying every woman he comes in contact with.

Be mindful and be safe. Protect you, your home, and your family at all cost. Be a woman who's respected by men, not selected by them to become a statistic. And remember, an unhealthy lifestyle is an unhealthy relationship.

KNOW YOUR STATUS

A new report from the U.S. Centers for Disease Control and Prevention says: Although progress has been made, black people in America are still being hit hard by HIV/AIDS.

The CDC study found that out of more than 12,200 black men and women diagnosed with HIV in 2004, nearly 22 percent had progressed to AIDS by the time they were diagnosed. That means diagnosis and treatment are often coming too late.

Of the Black Americans with HIV diagnosed in 2013, only about 54 percent were receiving continuous medical care. Of those receiving care, less than half had effectively suppressed the virus. This is far below the national HIV/AIDS strategy goals of 90 percent of HIV patients in treatment and 80 percent with undetectable HIV by 2020.

According to the report, from 2010 to 2014, the annual HIV diagnosis rate decreased for blacks by 16 percent. Yet, in 2015, black people still accounted for 45 percent of new HIV diagnosis.

Among black women, the annual rate of HIV diagnosis was about 16 times greater than the rate among white women. The findings also indicated that many black men might be infected with HIV for years without knowing it.

For people living with HIV, getting diagnosed and starting treatment early is an essential step toward long-term health. For more information on HIV/AIDS, visit the U.S. Centers for Disease Control and Prevention.

WORD PHRASES AND MEANINGS

Unscramble the words to reveal the meaning. Become more familiar with the gay terminology and the way it's used:

ETE .... Juicy information or a formal greeting

KLICEP .... Hideous or extremely ugly

KINSCING .... Hot, amazing, or flawless

HISF .... Female

YILL .... A fem guys penis

MHUNC .... To eat or suck

SKID .... Guy's or reference to the LGBTO community

TABE .... Flawless or on point

DESEVR .... Slayed or crushed the haters or competition

TOP .... Spreading rumors or lies

HASDY .... Two-faced or some timing

DRANG .... High class or elite

KCOEDLC.............................. Noticed or became aware of

UCNLKABOCLE..................... Unnoticeable or unaware of

RITWL..................... To have sex with or sexually play with

VILE ....Like, enjoy, or appreciate

TALSY.. Untrustworthy

OKOGED...Pranked or made fun of

IPECYE..Big or well-hung penis

ECAKY......................................Phat or plump ass

GUM .... Extremely handsome or beautiful

HASPE............................Curved or in great physical shape

DEIONC .... Well off or financially stable

HERFAT .... Husband or boyfriend

EIP.. Ass or booty

ECEIP .... A man's penis

SESMY .... Grimmy or suck

ERUTEAF...................................To like or be into someone

TACTY ....Feisty or full of attitude

CHECKLIST

I've created a checklist. (The is my man gay checklist) Read each question and answer it as honestly as possible. At the end of the checklist, add up each of the columns. Based on your answers, you'll be able to decide if you're sleeping with a gay man.

This checklist was created as an eye opener. It's also for fun as a brain teaser. So, let's check out ways to revealing your man's secret.

IS MY MAN GAY?

ANSWER:

Almost Always,

Sometimes,

Never

1. Does your man wear dark colored shades or glasses when out in public?

   _____

2. Is he known to have dirty fingernails?

   _____

3. Even though you're in a committed relationship, is he known to have condoms?

   _____

4. Does he arch, shape, design, or pluck his eyebrows?

   _____

5. Does he prefer anal sex more than vaginal sex?

   _____

6. Is he a fan of eating your ass?

_____

7. Does he like his salad tossed?

_____

8. Does he stay out late on Tuesday's or Thursday's?

_____

9. Does he have more than one cell phone?

_____

10. Has he ever gone on social media in front of you?

_____

11. Does he change clothes throughout the day?

_____

12. Has he ever asked or hinted that you suck him off from behind?

_____

13. Does he change the bed sheets without you asking him to?

_____

14. Is he known to have openly gay friends, male or female?

_____

15. Is his best friend or main man known to have influence over him?

_____

16. Is he known to hate or speak negative about homosexuals?

_____

17. Does his penis go soft during sex with you? Or takes time to rise?

_____

18. Does he shave his body? Armpits, legs, or pelvis?

_____

19. Is he a fan of using your hygiene products? Deo, body wash, etc?

_____

20. Is he known to go in and out of jail or prison?

_____

Almost Always Total: _____

Sometimes Total: _____

Never Total: _____

REVIEW QUESTIONS

1) If you walked in and caught your man having sex with another guy, how would you react?

2) Were you aware that a homosexual lifestyle consisted of so many different categories?

3) Do you feel men prefer to remain undercover because they're fearful of coming out due to rejection, or because they want their cake and eat it, too?

4) How do you feel about the opinion that a person is born gay? Do you agree that it's possible, or disagree and think it's a choice that one makes?

5) Can a man's insecurities possibly be a direct indication of his homosexuality?

6) Do you feel the only difference between a straight man and a gay man is a discreet opportunity?

7) Do you think it's possible to tell if your man is sleeping with another man based on his sexual performance in the bedroom?

8) Do you feel a man's aggressive behavior after being released from jail or prison is the result of him battling the urge while transitioning back into society?

9) Would testing your man sexuality by conducting a test on him be a good idea?

10) After reading this book do you suspect that you're possibly living or sleeping with an undercover man?

11) What's the word weakling a good word to describe men?

12) How do you feel about the biblical story of Adam and Eve? And was it appropriate concerning the topic?

13) What are your thoughts on the Ugly Truth? And women that are so desperately trying to keep a man, by willing to accept their homosexuality?

14) Do you feel that the real confessions from the men in the book gave you a better understanding inside the world of an undercover or down low man?

15) After reading this book do you think or feel that you are now a better judge of character and have the ability to distinguish a straight man from a gay man?

16) Do you feel the questions on the check list proves a man is GAY?

17) Do you feel that 90% of the men that has served a jail or prison sentence could have been sexually involved with another man while incarcerated?

18) What do you feel could have made this book better?

You may inbox me the answers to the review questions or ask any additional questions or information on how to tell if your man is gay. Submit your answers and questions to:

Demek_Levon@yahoo.com

or

instagram@demeklevon_HowToTellIfYourManIsGay.

ACKNOWLEDGMENTS

First, I want to thank God; without Your love and grace, nothing is possible. I've questioned You so many times because of the heavy burdens You have placed on my shoulders. Yet, I still trust in You and only You to lead me to greatness. Maybe this book is the light to my darkness.

Zakiya Clarkson, my beautiful niece, I could never physically explain the love I have for you in my heart. My love is so far beyond words. Your loyalty and support mean the world to me. I got you forever! Quiana Middleton, Big Sis, keep holding down the family in the absence of our Queen. I love you so much. Brother-in-law, Leroy, thanks for stepping up to the plate and being there for my family. Much respect.

Michael Morgan, thank you for your love and support during the hard times in my life. You have touched my life in ways you could never imagine. Your friendship is priceless. Love Dorsey @Ladylovemusic.com, you're a rare breed and one of the realist females on earth. Keep feeding them that mental food that only a selected few can digest. Thank you for being a friend and believing in me and my message.

Tabatha Maria, author of *My Life Isn't Pretty,* thank you for all the pointers and advice. I love you, cousin. Terria "Teetz" Mcaffee, you've been there from the beginning. How could I not love you for life? Akiba "nevergivingup" Prince, you know there's no way I could ever forget about you. I told you I was taking you with me, and I meant that. We met under the craziest circumstances, but our friendship grew into something worth treasuring. Loyalty is important to me, and you're one loyal friend. I love you to pieces.

Ayesha "Vessi" Kelly, my #1 fan. You have been in my corner from the very beginning. Continuing this journey without your support would be impossible. Brandon "Dubuy" Bennett, I must say "thank you" for putting a smile on my face during such a painful time in my life.

Special thanks to Henry Monroe, Jr. Your efforts to break me motivated me to go harder and be stronger. You tried to destroy my dreams, but you didn't succeed. The pain you inflicted on my heart changed me forever. I am who I am because of you. Thank you so much for bringing the truth to my words and inspiring my writing. Sorry, you weren't strong enough or loyal enough to stand tall until the end. Unlike you, the love in my heart is real and can never be replaced. I love you, today, tomorrow, and forever, and don't forget the afterlife.

Tiffany Miller, Towhyia Mcaffee, Timeka Ross, Bobby Mcaffee Jr., Tashawnia Mcaffee, Kendra "Pitt" Ross, Kyrstal Ross, Tyanna Butler, Tybren Butler, D'Angelo Richardson, Randall Strouse, Lorue "Shy" Frankline, Satin Harrison (I love you bae), Eric Heard, Eddie Douglas Jr., Darius "Tunchie" Strong, Christopher "Mr. 305" Bennett, Andrew "Eva" Gomez, Jasmine Butler, Josolyn Johnson, Carrise Walker, Ira Clark, Gwen Watson, Yola Griffin, Kala Murray and my girls and support team from Orlando, Florida, Nika Mincey, Tiffany Whitfield, and Precious Hall. Plus, the rest of my family, friends, and fans. Thank you so much for spreading the word and supporting this movement. I love you all and stay tuned; there's more to come.

Don't hold yourself responsible if one goes astray-

For your life you took responsibility and chose the route to sunnier days

Smiling because I've loved them all-

No shade thrown,

It's true, our relationship will help us evolve

I'm thankful for the friendships I've encountered along the way

Hate them? No!

* * *

That would be foolish, "Wouldn't you say?"

Following your dreams can sometimes leave others amiss,

Not everyone in your camp will be overjoyed with bliss.

Where I am today,

Has taken sacrifice, dedication and commitment in many ways

We all have a path which will lead us someday.

www.ingramcontent.com/pod-product-compliance
Lightning Source LLC
La Vergne TN
LVHW021501080426
835509LV00018B/2360